SkillBuilder

Grade 3

Math Workbook - 1

▸ *Operations and Algebraic Thinking*

Important Instruction

Students, Parents, and Teachers can use the URL or QR code provided below to access additional practice questions, educational videos, worksheets, mobile apps, standards information and more.

URL	QR Code
Visit the URL below and place the book access code http://www.lumoslearning.com/a/tedbooks **Access Code: G3MSBOA-60582-P**	

Contributing Author - Keyana M. Martinez
Contributing Author - LaSina McLain-Jackson
Executive Producer - Mukunda Krishnaswamy
Designer - Mirona Jova
Database Administrator - R. Raghavendra Rao

COPYRIGHT ©2018 by Lumos Information Services, LLC. **ALL RIGHTS RESERVED**. No part of this work covered by the copyright hereon may be reproduced or used in any form or by an means graphic, electronic, or mechanical, including photocopying, recording, taping, Web distribution or information storage and retrieval systems without the written permission of the publisher.

First Edition- 2020

ISBN-10: 1-940484-99-5

ISBN-13: 978-1-940484-99-0

Printed in the United States of America

For permissions and additional information contact us

Lumos Information Services, LLC
Email: support@lumoslearning.com

PO Box 1575
Piscataway, NJ 08855-1575
Tel: (732) 384-0146
Fax: (866) 283-6471

http://www.LumosLearning.com

Lumos Operations and Algebraic Thinking Skill Builder, Grade 3 - Multiplication and Division

This Book Includes:

- Practice questions to help students master
    - Operations and Algebraic Thinking
- Detailed answer explanations for every question
- Strategies for building speed and accuracy

Plus access to Online Workbooks which include:

- Instructional videos
- Mobile apps related to the learning objective
- Hundreds of additional practice questions
- Self-paced learning and personalized score reports
- Instant feedback after completion of the workbook

Table of Contents

Online Program Benefits	I
Introduction	1
How to use this book effectively	2

Operations and Algebraic Thinking   3

Understanding Multiplication	4
Understanding Division	14
Applying Multiplication & Division	20
Finding Unknown Values	26
Multiplication & Division Properties	32
Relating Multiplication & Division	38
Multiplication & Division Facts	45
Two-Step Problems	53
Number Patterns	59
Answer Key and Detailed Explanations	**65**

Additional Information   87

What if I buy more than one Lumos Study Program?	87
Lumos StepUp® Mobile App FAQ for Students	88
Lumos StepUp® Mobile App FAQ for Parents and Teachers	89
Common Core Standards Cross-reference Table	90

Online Program Benefits

Students*

- Rigorous Standards Practice
- Technology-enhanced item types practice
- Additional learning resources such as videos and apps

Parents*

- You can review your student's online work by login to your parent account
- Pinpoint student areas of difficulty
- Develop custom lessons & assignments
- Access to High-Quality Question Bank

Teachers*

- Review the online work of your students
- Get insightful student reports
- Discover standards aligned videos, apps and books through EdSearch
- Easily access standards information along with the Coherence Map
- Create and share information about your classroom or school events

* Terms and Conditions apply

URL	QR Code
Visit the URL below and place the book access code http://www.lumoslearning.com/a/tedbooks **Access Code: G3MSBOA-60582-P**	

Start using the online resources included with this book today!

Introduction

Books in the Lumos Skill Builder series are designed to help students master specific skills in Math and English Language Arts. The content of each workbook is rigorous and aligned with the robust standards. Each standard, and substandard, has its own specific content. Taking the time to study and practice each standard individually can help students more adequately understand and demonstrate proficiency of that standard in their particular grade level.

Unlike traditional printed books, this book provides online access to engaging educational videos, mobile apps and assessments. Blending printed resources with technology based learning tools and resources has proven to be an effective strategy to help students of the current generation master learning objectives. We call these books tedBooks™ since they connect printed books to a repository of online learning resources!

Additionally, students have individual strengths and weaknesses. Being able to practice content by standard allows them the ability to more deeply understand each standard and be able to work to strengthen academic weaknesses. The online resources create personalized learning opportunities for each student and provides immediate individualized feedback.

We believe that yearlong learning and adequate practice before the test are the keys to success on standardized tests. The books in the Skill Builder series will help students gain foundational skills needed to perform well on the standardized tests.

How to Use this Book Effectively

The Lumos Program is a flexible learning tool. It can be adapted to suit a student's skill level and the time available to practice. Here are some tips to help you use this book and the online resources effectively:

Students

- The standards in each book can be practiced in the order designed, or in the order of your own choosing.
- Answer all questions in each workbook.
- Use the online workbooks to further practice your areas of difficulty and complement classroom learning.
- Watch videos recommended for the lesson or question.
- Download and try mobile apps related to what you are learning.

Parents

- Get student reports and useful information about your school by downloading the Lumos SchoolUp™ app. Please follow directions provided in "How to download Lumos SchoolUp™ App" section of this chapter.
- Review your child's performance in the "Lumos Online Workbooks" periodically. You can do this by simply asking your child to log into the system online and selecting the subject area you wish to review.
- Review your child's work in each workbook.

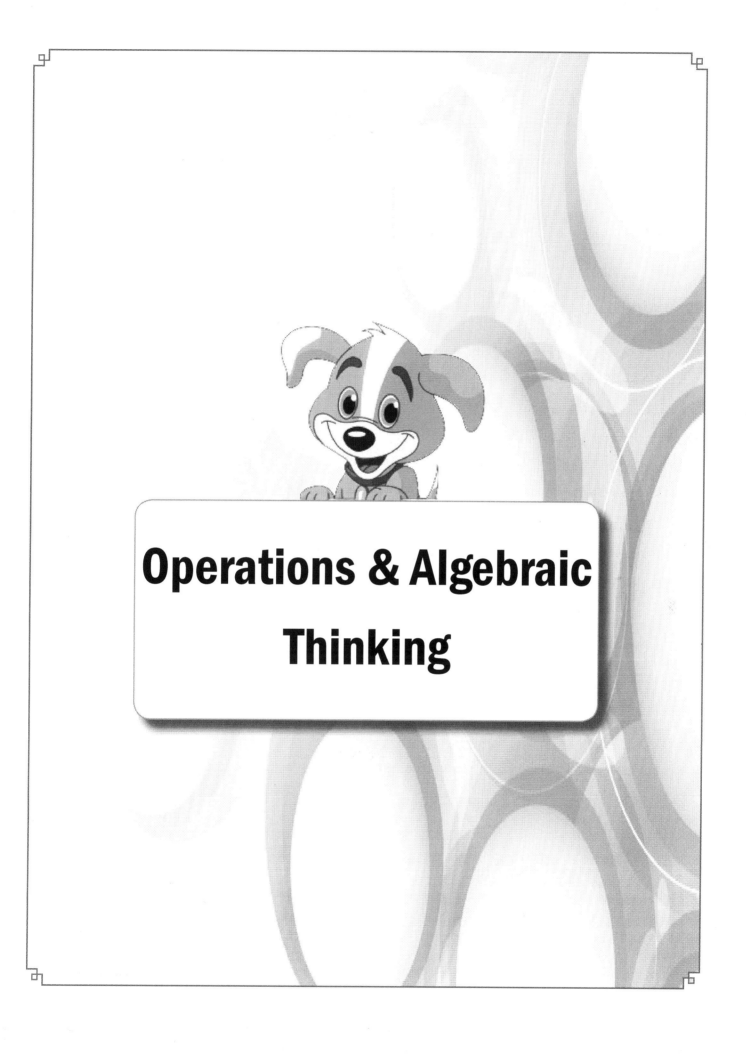

Understanding Multiplication

1. Which multiplication fact is being modeled below?

    ▱▱▱▱▱▱▱▱
    ▱▱▱▱▱▱▱▱
    ▱▱▱▱▱▱▱▱

    Ⓐ 3 x 10 = 30
    Ⓑ 4 x 10 = 40
    Ⓒ 4 x 9 = 36
    Ⓓ 3 x 9 = 27

2. Which numerical expression describes this array?

    ○○○○○
    ○○○○○
    ○○○○○
    ○○○○○

    Ⓐ 4 + 5
    Ⓑ 5 + 4
    Ⓒ 4 x 5
    Ⓓ 4 x 4

3. Which number sentence describes this array?

    ○○○○○○○
    ○○○○○○○
    ○○○○○○○
    ○○○○○○○

    Ⓐ 8 x 4 = 32
    Ⓑ 7 + 5 = 12
    Ⓒ 5 x 7 = 35
    Ⓓ 4 x 7 = 28

Name: _____   Date: _____

4. Which number sentence describes this array?

Ⓐ 2 x 12 = 24
Ⓑ 2 + 12 = 14
Ⓒ 12 + 2 = 24
Ⓓ 10 x 2 = 20

5. Identify the multiplication sentence for the picture below:

Ⓐ 4 x 4 = 16
Ⓑ 4 x 3 = 12
Ⓒ 3 x 4 = 12
Ⓓ 4 x 2 = 8

6. What multiplication fact does this picture model?

○○○○○○
○○○○○○
○○○○○○
○○○○○○

Ⓐ 4 x 6 = 24
Ⓑ 4 x 7 = 28
Ⓒ 6 x 3 = 18
Ⓓ 7 x 4 = 28

Name: _____ Date: _____

7. Identify the multiplication sentence for the picture below:

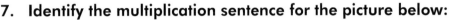

Ⓐ 7 x 2 = 14
Ⓑ 7 x 3 = 21
Ⓒ 7 x 4 = 28
Ⓓ 6 x 3 = 18

8. Identify the multiplication sentence for the picture below:

Ⓐ 4 x 4 = 16
Ⓑ 3 x 6 = 18
Ⓒ 3 x 4 = 12
Ⓓ 3 x 5 = 15

9. Identify the multiplication sentence for the picture below:

Ⓐ 3 x 2 = 6
Ⓑ 3 x 3 = 9
Ⓒ 4 x 2 = 8
Ⓓ 3 x 1 = 3

Name: _____   Date: _____

10. Identify the multiplication sentence for the picture below:

Ⓐ 3 x 5 = 15
Ⓑ 4 x 4 = 16
Ⓒ 5 x 4 = 20
Ⓓ 7 x 4 = 28

11. Identify the multiplication sentence for the picture below:

Ⓐ 2 x 5 = 10
Ⓑ 4 x 2 = 8
Ⓒ 4 x 1 = 4
Ⓓ 4 + 2 = 6

12. **Identify the multiplication sentence for the picture below:**

Ⓐ 6 x 7 = 42
Ⓑ 6 x 8 = 48
Ⓒ 8 x 9 = 72
Ⓓ 8 x 8 = 64

13. **Identify the multiplication sentence for the picture below:**

Ⓐ 10 x 1 = 10
Ⓑ 9 x 2 = 18
Ⓒ 2 x 10 = 20
Ⓓ 5 x 4 = 20

14. Identify the multiplication sentence for the picture below:

Ⓐ 5 x 5 = 25
Ⓑ 4 x 4 = 16
Ⓒ 4 x 6 = 24
Ⓓ 5 x 4 = 20

15. Identify the multiplication sentence for the picture below

Ⓐ 3 x 1 = 3
Ⓑ 5 x 3 = 15
Ⓒ 3 x 2 = 6
Ⓓ 3 x 3 = 9

16. Represent the below equation as a multiplication expression. Write your answer in the box below.

    8 + 8 + 8 + 8?

17. Match each multiplication statement to the correct addition statement by darkening the corresponding circles.

	Column A: 3+3+3+3+3+3	Column B: 3+3+3+3+3+3+3+3	Column C: 3+3+3
3 x 8	○	○	○
3 x 3	○	○	○
3 x 6	○	○	○

18. For each of the picture, write the correct mathematical expression in the box.

19. PART A

John finds the solution for 8 x 6 by solving for (8 x 5) + 8. Is John correct? Explain why you think that John's strategy is correct or not? Write your answer in the box below.

PART B

There are Seven boys, and each of them buys 6 pens. How many pens do they buy all together? Write an equation to represent this. Also, Find the total number of pens purchased using the equation.

Name: _____   Date: _____

20. Complete the following table:

Number of lions	5	6	9		
Total number of legs	20			32	16

NOTES

Name: _____   Date: _____   20

Understanding Division

1. George is canning pears. He has 100 pears and he divides the pears evenly among 10 pots. How many pears does George put in each pot?

    Ⓐ 9 pears
    Ⓑ 5 pears
    Ⓒ 8 pears
    Ⓓ 10 pears

2. Marisa made 15 woolen dolls. She gave the same number of woolen dolls to 3 friends. How many dolls did Marisa give to each friend?

    Ⓐ 4 woolen dolls
    Ⓑ 3 woolen dolls
    Ⓒ 5 woolen dolls
    Ⓓ 6 woolen dolls

3. Lisa bought 50 mangoes. She divided them equally into 5 basins. How many mangoes did Lisa put in each basin?

    Ⓐ 10 mangos
    Ⓑ 8 mangos
    Ⓒ 5 mangos
    Ⓓ 7 mangos

4. Jennifer picked 30 oranges from the basket. If it takes 6 oranges to make a one liter jar of juice, how many one liter jars of juice can Jennifer make?

    Ⓐ 4 jars
    Ⓑ 3 jars
    Ⓒ 6 jars
    Ⓓ 5 jars

5. Miller bought 80 rolls of paper towels. If there are 10 rolls of paper towels in each pack, how many packs of paper towels did Miller buy?

    Ⓐ 6 packs
    Ⓑ 8 packs
    Ⓒ 7 packs
    Ⓓ 5 packs

6. James takes 15 photographs of his school building. He gave the same number of photographs to 5 friends. How many photographs did James give to each friend?

   Ⓐ 2 photographs
   Ⓑ 3 photographs
   Ⓒ 6 photographs
   Ⓓ 5 photographs

7. Ron took 81 playing cards and arranged them into 9 equal piles. How many playing cards did Ron put in each pile?

   Ⓐ 5 playing cards
   Ⓑ 4 playing cards
   Ⓒ 6 playing cards
   Ⓓ 9 playing cards

8. Robert wants to buy 40 ice cream cups from the ice cream parlor. If there are 10 ice cream cups in each box, how many boxes of ice cream cups should Robert buy?

   Ⓐ 6 boxes
   Ⓑ 3 boxes
   Ⓒ 4 boxes
   Ⓓ 5 boxes

9. Marilyn wants to purchase 20 tiles. If the tiles come in packs of 5, how many packs should Marilyn buy?

   Ⓐ 3 packs
   Ⓑ 4 packs
   Ⓒ 5 packs
   Ⓓ 6 packs

10. There are 30 people running around the path. If the runners are evenly divided among the path's 5 lanes, how many people are running in each lane?

    Ⓐ 6 runners
    Ⓑ 5 runners
    Ⓒ 8 runners
    Ⓓ 4 runners

11. Sally is buying goodie bags for her class. She needs 24 bags in all. If the bags come in packs of 3, how many packs does Sally need?

    Ⓐ 21 packs
    Ⓑ 3 packs
    Ⓒ 24 packs
    Ⓓ 8 packs

12. Mr. Johnson is planting a garden. He wants to use all of his 44 seeds and wants to make 4 rows of vegetables. How many seeds should he plant in each row?

    Ⓐ 22 seeds
    Ⓑ 11 seeds
    Ⓒ 4 seeds
    Ⓓ 88 seeds

13. Destiny, Jimmy, and Marcy have 32 marbles all together. Tommy adds 4 marbles to the set. If the group of friends wants to evenly divide the marbles so that each person has the same number, how many marbles should each person receive?

    Ⓐ 4 marbles
    Ⓑ 8 marbles
    Ⓒ 9 marbles
    Ⓓ 10 marbles

14. Mr. Baker earned $100 for five days of work. If he made the same amount each day, how much money did he make per day?

    Ⓐ $15 per day
    Ⓑ $20 per day
    Ⓒ $25 per day
    Ⓓ $30 per day

15. Seth and his brother have collected 26 seashells on the beach. If they want to share them equally, how many seashells will each of them receive?

    Ⓐ 6 seashells
    Ⓑ 9 seashells
    Ⓒ 26 seashells
    Ⓓ 13 seashells

16. A pizza is cut into 8 slices. Tim and Kira want to share the pizza. If they both eat the same number of slices, how many slices will each person eat? Write it in the box given below.

17. Gabriela has 16 stickers. She wants to find two ways to divide the stickers into equal groups. Which expressions can she use to divide the stickers? Mark all the correct answers.

    Ⓐ 16 ÷ 2
    Ⓑ 16 ÷ 3
    Ⓒ 16 ÷ 4
    Ⓓ 16 ÷ 5

18. Circle the picture that shows the expression 10 ÷ 5.

Ⓐ

Ⓑ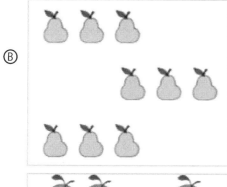

Ⓒ

Name: _____   Date: _____

19. Miriam has 100 marbles. She wants to divide the marbles into equal groups. How many ways can she do this? Complete the table by listing all the possible ways in which you can divide 100. Write the missing numbers and fill the table. Enter the numbers in ascending order.

Dividend	Possible Divisors
100	2
100	4
100	
100	
100	20
100	25
100	

20. For each expression below, choose the correct symbol to be filled in the blank.

	<	>	=
30 ÷ 5 ___ 42 ÷ 6	○	○	○
72 ÷ 8 ___ 63 ÷ 7	○	○	○
54 ÷ 6 ___ 56 ÷ 7	○	○	○

Online Resources: Understanding Division

URL	QR Code
http://lumoslearning.com/a/m13345	

 Videos   Apps   Sample Questions

NOTES

Name: _____ Date: _____

20

Applying Multiplication & Division

1. 54 x 3 = ?
   The product in this number sentence is _____.

   Ⓐ 54
   Ⓑ 162
   Ⓒ 3
   Ⓓ 54 and 3

2. A Snack Shop has twice as many popcorn balls as they do cotton candy. If there are 30 popcorn balls, how many cotton candies are there?

   Ⓐ 7
   Ⓑ 450
   Ⓒ 30
   Ⓓ 15

3. Monica has 56 DVDs in her movie collection. This is 8 times as many as Sue has. How many DVDs does Sue have?

   Ⓐ 8
   Ⓑ 6
   Ⓒ 7
   Ⓓ 10

4. Jonathan can do 7 jumping jacks. Marcus can do 4 times as many as Jonathan. How many jumping jacks can Marcus do?

   Ⓐ 28
   Ⓑ 8
   Ⓒ 4
   Ⓓ 7

5. Darren has seen 4 movies this year. Marsha has seen 3 times as many movies as Darren. How many movies has Marsha seen?

   Ⓐ 7
   Ⓑ 3
   Ⓒ 4
   Ⓓ 12

6. Sarah is planting a garden. She will plant 4 rows with 9 seeds in each row. How many plants will be in the garden?

   Ⓐ 32 plants
   Ⓑ 36 plants
   Ⓒ 42 plants
   Ⓓ 13 plants

7. Mrs. Huerta's class is having a pizza party. There are 24 students in the class. Each pizza has 12 slices. How many pizzas does Mrs. Huerta need to order for each child to have 1 slice?

   Ⓐ 3 pizzas
   Ⓑ 2 pizzas
   Ⓒ 1 pizza
   Ⓓ 4 pizzas

8. There are 27 apples. How many pies can be made if each pie uses 3 apples?

   Ⓐ 7 pies
   Ⓑ 8 pies
   Ⓒ 9 pies
   Ⓓ 10 pies

9. Keegan is planting a garden in even rows. He has 48 seeds. Which layout is NOT possible?

   Ⓐ 6 rows of 8 seeds
   Ⓑ 8 rows of 6 seeds
   Ⓒ 7 rows of 7 seeds
   Ⓓ 12 rows of 4 seeds

10. There are 25 students in a gym class. They want to play a game with 5 equal teams. How many students will be on each team?

    Ⓐ 4 students
    Ⓑ 5 students
    Ⓒ 7 students
    Ⓓ 3 students

Name: _____   Date: _____

11. Josie has 7 days to read a book with 21 chapters. How many chapters should she read each day?

    Ⓐ 3 chapters
    Ⓑ 4 chapters
    Ⓒ 5 chapters
    Ⓓ 7 chapters

12. Devon has $40 to spend on fuel. One gallon of fuel costs $5. How many gallons can Devon afford to buy?

    Ⓐ 5 gallons
    Ⓑ 12 gallons
    Ⓒ 9 gallons
    Ⓓ 8 gallons

13. Amanda is using the following cake recipe:
    4 cups flour
    1 cup sugar
    3 cups milk
    1 egg
    If Amanda needs to make three batches, how many cups of flour will she need?

    Ⓐ 7 cups
    Ⓑ 12 cups
    Ⓒ 10 cups
    Ⓓ 16 cups

14. Kim invited 20 friends to her birthday party. Twice as many friends than she invited showed up the day of the party. Which number sentence could be used to solve how many friends came to the party?

    Ⓐ n + 20 = 2
    Ⓑ n x 20 = 2
    Ⓒ 20 x 2 = n
    Ⓓ 20 - n = 20

Name: _____ Date: _____

15. The product of 9 and a number is 45.
    Which number sentence models this situation?

    Ⓐ 9 + n = 45
    Ⓑ 45 + 9 = n
    Ⓒ 9 x n = 45
    Ⓓ 5 x n = 45

16. A classroom has 5 rows of desks. There are 6 desks in each row. How many desks are there altogether? Select the number sentences that represent the solution. Choose all correct answers.

    Ⓐ 6 - 5 = 1
    Ⓑ 5 x 6 = 30
    Ⓒ 6 x 5 = 30
    Ⓓ 5 + 6 = 11

17. Jasmine bought a bouquet of 24 flowers. She plans to give the same number of flowers to her 4 friends, Daniel, Raquel, Elliot and Sue. How many flowers will each friend receive? Circle the correct answer.

    Ⓐ 2
    Ⓑ 5
    Ⓒ 6
    Ⓓ 4

18. There are 48 cupcakes to be shared equally among 6 boys. How many cupcakes will each boy get? Write your answer in the box given below.

19. PART A
    Fill in the blank with the correct symbol to make this equation true.

    64 ÷ 8 = 2 ___ 4.

    PART B
    Fill in the blank with the correct symbol to make this equation true.

    2 ___ 4 = 42 ÷ 7.

Name: _____ Date: _____

20. Joseph reads 8 pages every day. In how many days will he be able to complete reading a book which has 56 pages? Write an equation to represent this in the box below, and find the number of days Joseph takes to complete the book.

Online Resources: Applying Multiplication and Division

URL	QR Code
http://lumoslearning.com/a/m13425	

Videos   Apps   Sample Questions

NOTES

Finding Unknown Values

1. Find the number that makes this equation true.
   n x 6 = 30

   Ⓐ n = 11
   Ⓑ n = 7
   Ⓒ n = 5
   Ⓓ n = 3

2. Find the number that makes this equation true.
   7 x ___ = 21

   Ⓐ 3
   Ⓑ 4
   Ⓒ 5
   Ⓓ 6

3. Find the number that makes this equation true.
   ___ x 4 = 36

   Ⓐ 9
   Ⓑ 8
   Ⓒ 7
   Ⓓ 6

4. Find the number that makes this equation true.
   n ÷ 9 = 8

   Ⓐ n = 81
   Ⓑ n = 45
   Ⓒ n = 72
   Ⓓ n = 63

5. Find the number that makes this equation true.
   ___ ÷ 3 = 10

   Ⓐ 27
   Ⓑ 30
   Ⓒ 33
   Ⓓ 60

Name: _____   Date: _____

6. Find the number that makes this equation true.
   $45 \div n = 9$

   Ⓐ n = 10
   Ⓑ n = 7
   Ⓒ n = 5
   Ⓓ n = 3

7. Find the number that makes this equation true.
   $64 = \_\_\_ \times 8$

   Ⓐ 6
   Ⓑ 7
   Ⓒ 8
   Ⓓ 9

8. Find the number that makes this equation true.
   $12 \div \_\_\_ = 2$

   Ⓐ 7
   Ⓑ 6
   Ⓒ 8
   Ⓓ 4

9. Find the number that makes this equation true.
   $\_\_\_ \div 7 = 11$

   Ⓐ 63
   Ⓑ 70
   Ⓒ 77
   Ⓓ 78

10. Find the number that makes this equation true.
    $16 = n \times 4$

    Ⓐ n = 12
    Ⓑ n = 4
    Ⓒ n = 3
    Ⓓ n = 2

Name: _____ Date: _____

11. For what value of m is this equation true?
    m x 7 = 56

    Ⓐ m = 6
    Ⓑ m = 8
    Ⓒ m = 7
    Ⓓ m = 12

12. For what value of n is this equation true?
    60 ÷ n = 5

    Ⓐ n = 8
    Ⓑ n = 12
    Ⓒ n = 14
    Ⓓ n = 16

13. For what value of z is this equation true?
    9 x z = 81

    Ⓐ z = 11
    Ⓑ z = 9
    Ⓒ z = 12
    Ⓓ z = 7

14. For what value of p is this equation true?
    p ÷ 3 = 3

    Ⓐ p = 6
    Ⓑ p = 1
    Ⓒ p = 9
    Ⓓ p = 0

15. For what value of u is this equation true?
    10 ÷ u = 10

    Ⓐ u = 1
    Ⓑ u = 0
    Ⓒ u = 10
    Ⓓ u = 100

16. ___ ÷ 6 = 9

Which number makes the equation true? Write your answer in the box given.

17. ___ x ___ = 14

Which numbers will make the equation true? Select all correct answers.

Ⓐ 5
Ⓑ 7
Ⓒ 6
Ⓓ 2

18. Enter the correct answer in the table.

Equation	Product
4 x 8 =	
	x 7 = 63
3 x 5 =	
	x 1 = 7

19. PART A

A pen costs $7 to buy. How much would six pens cost? Write an equation to represent this in the box below.

Name: _____   Date: _____

19. PART B

Use the equation from PART A to find the cost of six pens.

20. Match the value of n for each of the equations given.

Equation	n=7	n=6
3 × 8 = 4 × n	○	○
72 ÷ 9 = 56 ÷ n	○	○

Online Resources: Finding Unknown Values

URL	QR Code
http://lumoslearning.com/a/m13424	

Videos   Apps   Sample Questions

NOTES

Multiplication & Division Properties

1. Which of these statements is not true?

    Ⓐ 4 x (3 x 6) = (4 x 3) x 6
    Ⓑ 4 x 3 = 3 x 4
    Ⓒ 15 x 0 = 0 x 15
    Ⓓ 12 x 1 = 12 x 12

2. Which of these statements is true?

    Ⓐ The product of 11 x 6 is equal to the product of 6 x 11.
    Ⓑ The product of 11 x 6 is greater than the product of 6 x 11.
    Ⓒ The product of 11 x 6 is less than the product of 6 x 11.
    Ⓓ There is no relationship between the product of 11 x 6 and the product of 6 x 11.

3. Which of the following expressions has a value of 0?

    Ⓐ (3 x 4) x 1
    Ⓑ 50 x 1
    Ⓒ 3 x 4 x 0
    Ⓓ (3 x 1) x 2

4. Select the option in which both the numerical expressions result in a value of 0?

    Ⓐ 60 x 1 and 1 x 60
    Ⓑ 10 x 10 and 0 x 10
    Ⓒ 27 x 0 and 0 x 27
    Ⓓ 0 ÷ 15 and 15 ÷ 15

5. Which mathematical property does this equation model?
    6 x 1 = 6

    Ⓐ Commutative Property of Multiplication
    Ⓑ Associative Property of Multiplication
    Ⓒ Identity Property of Multiplication
    Ⓓ Distributive Property

Name: _____   Date: _____

6. Which mathematical property does this equation model?
   9 x 6 = 6 x 9

   Ⓐ Commutative Property of Multiplication
   Ⓑ Associative Property of Multiplication
   Ⓒ Identity Property of Multiplication
   Ⓓ Distributive Property

7. Which mathematical property does this equation model?
   (2 x 10) x 3 = 2 x (10 x 3)

   Ⓐ Commutative Property of Multiplication
   Ⓑ Associative Property of Multiplication
   Ⓒ Identity Property of Multiplication
   Ⓓ Distributive Property

8. Which mathematical property does this equation model?
   4 x (9 + 6) = (4 x 9) + (4 x 6)

   Ⓐ Commutative Property of Multiplication
   Ⓑ Associative Property of Multiplication
   Ⓒ Identity Property of Multiplication
   Ⓓ Distributive Property

9. By the Commutative Property of Multiplication, if you know that 4 x 5= 20, then you also know that _____ .

   Ⓐ 20 is an even number
   Ⓑ 4 x 6 = 24
   Ⓒ 5 x 4 = 20
   Ⓓ 5 is greater than 4

10. By the Associative Property of Multiplication, If you know that (2 x 3) x 4 = 24, then you also know that _____.

    Ⓐ 2 x (3 x 4) = 24
    Ⓑ 2 x 4 = 8
    Ⓒ 24 ÷ 6 = 4
    Ⓓ (2 x 3) x 5 = 30

Name: _____ Date: _____

11. Complete the following statement:
    Multiplication and _____ are inverse operations.

    Ⓐ addition
    Ⓑ subtraction
    Ⓒ division
    Ⓓ distribution

12. 32 x 7 = 7 x 32
    This equation models the _____.

    Ⓐ Commutative Property of Multiplication
    Ⓑ Associative Property of Multiplication
    Ⓒ Identity Property of Multiplication
    Ⓓ Distributive Property

13. 26 x 2 = (20 x 2) + (6 x 2)
    This equation models the _____ .

    Ⓐ Commutative Property of Multiplication
    Ⓑ Associative Property of Multiplication
    Ⓒ Identity Property of Multiplication
    Ⓓ Distributive Property

14. By the Identity Property of Multiplication, you know that _____.

    Ⓐ 2 x 2 = 4
    Ⓑ 0 x 0 = 0
    Ⓒ 6 x 1 = 6
    Ⓓ 5 ÷ 5 = 1

15. What number belongs in the blank?
    10 x __ = 10

    Ⓐ 1
    Ⓑ 0
    Ⓒ 10
    Ⓓ 5

16. From the below 4 options, select 2 options that will result in the same product based on the commutative property of multiplication?

    Ⓐ 5 + 4
    Ⓑ 10 x 2
    Ⓒ 5 x 4
    Ⓓ 4 x 5

17. Make the equation true according to the Identity Property of Multiplication. Write the correct number in the answer box given below.

    7 x ___ = 7

18. (2 x 3) x 4 = 24 and 2 x (3 x 4) = 24

    Identify the property that is applicable. Circle the correct answer choice.

    Ⓐ Associative property of multiplication
    Ⓑ Distributive property
    Ⓒ Commutative property of multiplication
    Ⓓ Identity Property of Multiplication

19. PART A:

    Which number will make the below equation true. Write your answer in the box given below.

    3 x 7 = 7 x ?

    PART B:

    Which property did you use in Part A to arrive at the answer. Write the name of the property in the box given below.

Name: _____   Date: _____

20. Match the property with the correct example.

	3 x (5 x 7) = (3 x 5) x 7	3 x 1 = 3	3 x 5 = 5 x 3	3 x (5 + 7) = (3 x 5) + (3 x 7)
Commutative Property	○	○	○	○
Associative Property	○	○	○	○
Identity Property	○	○	○	○
Distributive Property	○	○	○	○

Online Resources: Multiplication & Division Properties

URL	QR Code
http://lumoslearning.com/a/m13426	

 Videos   Apps   Sample Questions

NOTES

Name: _____ Date: _____

Relating Multiplication & Division

1. Find the number that would complete both of the following number sentences.
   ___ x 6 = 30
   30 ÷ 6 = ___

   Ⓐ 7
   Ⓑ 5
   Ⓒ 6
   Ⓓ 24

2. Find the number that would complete both of the following number sentences.
   7 x ___ = 21
   21 ÷ ___ = 7

   Ⓐ 5
   Ⓑ 14
   Ⓒ 3
   Ⓓ 7

3. Find the number that would complete both of the following number sentences.
   72 ÷ ___ = 8
   8 x ___ = 72

   Ⓐ 8
   Ⓑ 9
   Ⓒ 10
   Ⓓ 64

4. Find the number that would complete both of the following number sentences.
   50 ÷ ___ = 5
   ___ x 5 = 50

   Ⓐ 15
   Ⓑ 5
   Ⓒ 45
   Ⓓ 10

Name: _____   Date: _____

5. Find the number that would complete both of the following number sentences.
   36 ÷ ___ =
   ___ x 9 = 36

   Ⓐ 4
   Ⓑ 5
   Ⓒ 27
   Ⓓ 9

6. There are 9 students in a group. Each student needs 5 sheets of paper to complete a project. Which number sentence below can be used to find out how many total sheets of paper are needed for this project? Select all the correct answer choices.

   Ⓐ 5 x ___ = 9
   Ⓑ 9 x 5 = ___
   Ⓒ ___ ÷ 5 = 9
   Ⓓ 9 ÷ 5 = ___

7. In a football game, Timmy scored 8 touchdowns. Each touchdown was worth 7 points. Which number sentence below can be used to find out how many points Timmy scored in all?

   Ⓐ 56 x ___ = 8
   Ⓑ ___ ÷ 7 = 8
   Ⓒ 7 x 56 = ___
   Ⓓ 8 ÷ 7 = ___

8. Devon needs to buy 96 pencils for his goodie bags. Pencils are sold in packages of 12. Which number sentence below can be used to find out how many packages Devon needs to buy?

   Ⓐ 12 ÷ 96 = ___
   Ⓑ 12 x 96 = ___
   Ⓒ ___ x 12 = 96
   Ⓓ 12 ÷ ___ = 96

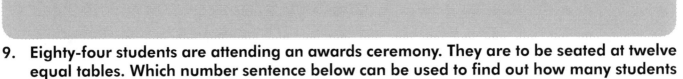

9. Eighty-four students are attending an awards ceremony. They are to be seated at twelve equal tables. Which number sentence below can be used to find out how many students should be assigned to each table?

   Ⓐ 6 x ____ = 84
   Ⓑ 12 x ____ = 84
   Ⓒ 84 x 12 = ____
   Ⓓ 12 ÷ 84 = ____

10. Walter has 16 slices of pizza to share among himself and seven friends. He wants each person to get an equal number of slices. Which number sentence below can be used to find out how many slices each person will get?

    Ⓐ 7 ÷ 16 = ____
    Ⓑ 7 x 16 = ____
    Ⓒ 7 x ____ = 16
    Ⓓ 8 x ____ = 16

11. Which of the following equations would be in the same fact family as:
    6 x 5 = 30?

    Ⓐ 30 ÷ 10 = 3
    Ⓑ 6 x 30 = 5
    Ⓒ 30 ÷ 5 = 6
    Ⓓ 5 ÷ 30 = 6

12. Which number sentence is equivalent to the number sentence below?
    4 x n = 32

    Ⓐ 4 x 32 = n
    Ⓑ n + 4 = 32
    Ⓒ 32 ÷ 4 = n
    Ⓓ 4 x 4 = n

13. Which number sentence is equivalent to the number sentence below?
    n x 6 = 48

    Ⓐ 48 x n = 6
    Ⓑ 6 x 4 = n
    Ⓒ 48 x 6 = n
    Ⓓ 48 ÷ n = 6

14. Which number sentence is equivalent to the number sentence below?
    45 ÷ n = 9

    Ⓐ 9 x 45 = n
    Ⓑ 45 x n = 9
    Ⓒ 9 x n = 45
    Ⓓ n + 9 = 45

15. David receives 2 pieces of candy for each chore that he completes each week. This week he earned 32 pieces of candy. Which number sentence below can be used to figure out how many chores David completed?

    Ⓐ 2 x 32 = ___
    Ⓑ ___ x 2 = 32
    Ⓒ 32 + 2 = ___
    Ⓓ 2 ÷ 32 = ___

16. Match each multiplication sentence with the corresponding division sentence. Remember, if a x b= c then c ÷ a= b.

	40÷5=8	36÷6=6	21÷7=3	18÷9=2
6 x 6= 36	○	○	○	○
9 x 2= 18	○	○	○	○
5 x 8= 40	○	○	○	○
7 x 3= 21	○	○	○	○

17. Complete the table by typing in the correct number. Remember, if a x b= c then c ÷ a= b.

	Division Expression	Quotient
If 4 x 4= 16 then...	16 ÷ 4=	
If 7 x 6= 42 then... 42 ÷		6
If 3 x 9= 27 then...		÷ 3=9

Name: _____ Date: _____

18. Which multiplication sentences relate to 63 ÷ 9 = 7? Select all the correct answers.
    Note: More than one option may be correct.

    Ⓐ 7 x 7 = 49
    Ⓑ 7 x 9 = 63
    Ⓒ 9 x 7 = 63
    Ⓓ 9 x 8 = 72

19. Which number sentence is equivalent to the number sentence below:

    65 ÷ n = 5.

    Ⓐ 65 = 5 × n
    Ⓑ 65 = 5 ÷ n
    Ⓒ 65 = n ÷ 5
    Ⓓ 65 = 5 - n

20. Part A

    For the expression below, Circle the correct symbol to be filled in the blank.

    40 ÷ 5 ___ 54 ÷ 9

    Ⓐ =
    Ⓑ >
    Ⓒ <

    Part B

    For the expression below, Circle the correct symbol to be filled in the blank.

    35 ÷ 7 ___ 28 ÷ 4

    Ⓐ =
    Ⓑ >
    Ⓒ <

Name: _____ Date: _____

Part C

For the expression below, Circle the correct symbol to be filled in the blank.

18 ÷ 6 ____ 24 ÷ 8

Ⓐ =
Ⓑ >
Ⓒ <

Online Resources: Relating Multiplication and Division

URL	QR Code
http://lumoslearning.com/a/m13427	

 Videos   Apps   Sample Questions

NOTES

Multiplication & Division Facts

1. Find the product.
   6 x 0 = ___

   Ⓐ 6
   Ⓑ 1
   Ⓒ 0
   Ⓓ 2

2. Find the product.
   1 x 10 = ___

   Ⓐ 0
   Ⓑ 1
   Ⓒ 10
   Ⓓ 11

3. Solve.
   3 x 8 = ___

   Ⓐ 24
   Ⓑ 21
   Ⓒ 18
   Ⓓ 28

4. Solve.
   ___ = 5 x 9

   Ⓐ 40
   Ⓑ 45
   Ⓒ 50
   Ⓓ 35

5. Find the product of 8 and 6.

   Ⓐ 14
   Ⓑ 42
   Ⓒ 48
   Ⓓ 56

Name: _____   Date: _____

6. Find the product of 7 and 7.

   Ⓐ 42
   Ⓑ 46
   Ⓒ 49
   Ⓓ 56

7. Find the product of 4 and 6.

   Ⓐ 20
   Ⓑ 24
   Ⓒ 28
   Ⓓ 32

8. Find the product.
   6 x 9 = ___

   Ⓐ 54
   Ⓑ 45
   Ⓒ 48
   Ⓓ 64

9. Find the product.
   ___ = 9 x 8

   Ⓐ 64
   Ⓑ 72
   Ⓒ 81
   Ⓓ 82

10. Which expression below has a product of 48?

    Ⓐ 6 x 7
    Ⓑ 4 x 14
    Ⓒ 7 x 8
    Ⓓ 8 x 6

11. Find the quotient of 25 and 5.

    Ⓐ 20
    Ⓑ 5
    Ⓒ 4
    Ⓓ 15

Name: _____ Date: _____

12. What is 32 divided by 4?

    Ⓐ 9
    Ⓑ 8
    Ⓒ 7
    Ⓓ 6

13. What is 28 divided by 7?

    Ⓐ 4
    Ⓑ 5
    Ⓒ 3
    Ⓓ 6

14. Find the quotient.
    0 ÷ 5 = ____

    Ⓐ 0
    Ⓑ 1
    Ⓒ 5
    Ⓓ 50

15. Find the quotient.
    7 ÷ 1 = ____

    Ⓐ 1
    Ⓑ 0
    Ⓒ 7
    Ⓓ 8

16. Find the quotient.
    ____ = 12 ÷ 2

    Ⓐ 9
    Ⓑ 8
    Ⓒ 7
    Ⓓ 6

Name: _____ Date: _____

17. Divide.
   63 ÷ 9 = ___

   Ⓐ 6
   Ⓑ 7
   Ⓒ 8
   Ⓓ 9

18. Divide.
   42 ÷ 7 = ___

   Ⓐ 5
   Ⓑ 6
   Ⓒ 7
   Ⓓ 8

19. Find the quotient of 33 and 3.

   Ⓐ 11
   Ⓑ 12
   Ⓒ 10
   Ⓓ 9

20. Divide.
   56 ÷ 7 = ___

   Ⓐ 6
   Ⓑ 7
   Ⓒ 8
   Ⓓ 9

21. Solve.
   4 x 12 = ____

   Ⓐ 36
   Ⓑ 48
   Ⓒ 42
   Ⓓ 46

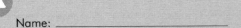

Name: _____   Date: _____

22. Solve.
   ___ = 75 ÷ 5

   Ⓐ 13
   Ⓑ 15
   Ⓒ 17
   Ⓓ 25

23. Solve.
   84 ÷ 12 = ___

   Ⓐ 7
   Ⓑ 8
   Ⓒ 9
   Ⓓ 12

24. Solve.
   12 x 3 = ___

   Ⓐ 32
   Ⓑ 36
   Ⓒ 39
   Ⓓ 48

25. Solve.
   36 ÷ 3 = ___

   Ⓐ 22
   Ⓑ 12
   Ⓒ 14
   Ⓓ 18

26. Solve.
   60 ÷ 5 = ___

   Ⓐ 8
   Ⓑ 9
   Ⓒ 12
   Ⓓ 14

Name: _____ Date: _____

27. Solve.
   11 x 4 = ___

   Ⓐ 32
   Ⓑ 44
   Ⓒ 39
   Ⓓ 46

28. Solve.
   ___ = 80 ÷ 8

   Ⓐ 10
   Ⓑ 9
   Ⓒ 8
   Ⓓ 12

29. Solve.
   12 x 8 = ___

   Ⓐ 72
   Ⓑ 84
   Ⓒ 92
   Ⓓ 96

30. Solve.
   50 ÷ 5 = ___

   25
   20
   10
   50

31. Match each equation to the correct product.

	12	18	32
6 x 3=	○	○	○
8 x 4=	○	○	○
4 x 3=	○	○	○
9 x 2=	○	○	○

Name: _____   Date: _____

32. 24 ÷ 4 = ?
    Write the answer in the box given below.

    ☐

33. Which expressions have a product of 36. Select all the correct answers.

    Ⓐ 6 x 6
    Ⓑ 8 x 4
    Ⓒ 6 x 8
    Ⓓ 9 x 4

34. Find the quotient. 27 ÷ 9 = ? Circle the correct answer.

    Ⓐ 18
    Ⓑ 4
    Ⓒ 3
    Ⓓ 2

35. Complete the following table.

5	x	8	=	
8	÷		=	8
	÷	7	=	0
6	x		=	30

Online Resources: Multiplication and Division Facts

URL	QR Code
http://lumoslearning.com/a/m13428	

 Videos   Apps   Sample Questions

NOTES

Two-Step Problems

1. Danny has 47 baseball cards. He gives his brother 11 cards. Danny then divides the remaining cards between 3 of his classmates. How many cards does each classmate receive?

   Ⓐ 15
   Ⓑ 3
   Ⓒ 12
   Ⓓ 11

2. Two classes of grade three students are lined up outside. One class is lined up in 3 rows of 7. The other class is lined up in 4 rows of 5. How many total third graders are lined up outside?

   Ⓐ 19 third graders
   Ⓑ 21 third graders
   Ⓒ 41 third graders
   Ⓓ 20 third graders

3. Jessica earns 10 dollars per hour for babysitting. She has saved 60 dollars so far. How many more hours will she need to babysit to buy something that costs 100 dollars?

   Ⓐ 40 hours
   Ⓑ 6 hours
   Ⓒ 10 hours
   Ⓓ 4 hours

4. George started with 2 bags of 10 cookies. He gave 12 cookies to his parents. How many cookies does George have now?

   Ⓐ 8 cookies
   Ⓑ 10 cookies
   Ⓒ 12 cookies
   Ⓓ 20 cookies

5. Renae has 60 minutes to do her chores and do her homework. She has 3 chores to complete and each chore takes 15 minutes to complete. After completing her chores, how many minutes does Renae have left to do her homework?

   Ⓐ 15 minutes
   Ⓑ 45 minutes
   Ⓒ 30 minutes
   Ⓓ 0 minutes

LumosLearning.com

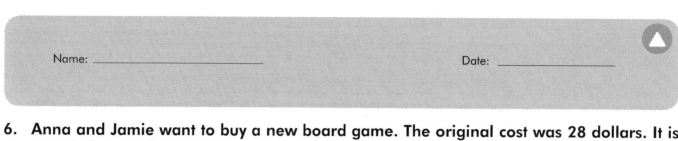

6. Anna and Jamie want to buy a new board game. The original cost was 28 dollars. It is on sale for 4 dollars off. How much money should each girl pay if they buy the game on sale and pay equal amounts?

   Ⓐ $24
   Ⓑ $2
   Ⓒ $12
   Ⓓ $14

7. 100 students went on a field trip. Ten students rode with their parents in a car while the remaining students were divided equally into 5 buses. How many students rode on each bus?

   Ⓐ 9 students
   Ⓑ 18 students
   Ⓒ 50 students
   Ⓓ 90 students

8. Julia has 32 books. Her sister has twice the number of books that Julia has. How many books do the girls have altogether?

   Ⓐ 66 books
   Ⓑ 32 books
   Ⓒ 64 books
   Ⓓ 96 books

9. Alicia bought 5 crates of apples. Each crate had 8 apples. She divided the apples equally into 10 bags. How many apples were in each bag?

   Ⓐ 40 apples
   Ⓑ 4 apples
   Ⓒ 10 apples
   Ⓓ 5 apples

10. Janeth went to the store and spent 4 dollars on markers. She also bought 3 copies of the same book. If she spent a total of 19 dollars, how much did each book cost?

    Ⓐ 5 dollars
    Ⓑ 4 dollars
    Ⓒ 3 dollars
    Ⓓ 6 dollars

11. Brian won 24 candy bars in a contest. He gave 2 candy bars to each of his 7 friends. How many candy bars does Brian have left?

   Ⓐ 14 candy bars
   Ⓑ 12 candy bars
   Ⓒ 10 candy bars
   Ⓓ 17 candy bars

12. Jenine gave 3 mini cupcakes to each of her three sisters. She then had 4 left for herself. How many mini cupcakes did Jenine start with?

   Ⓐ 13 mini cupcakes
   Ⓑ 9 mini cupcakes
   Ⓒ 10 mini cupcakes
   Ⓓ 7 mini cupcakes

13. Twenty-two people visited the art exhibit at the museum on Friday. Twice as many people visited on Saturday. How many people combined visited the art exhibit at the museum on Friday and Saturday?

   Ⓐ 88 people
   Ⓑ 66 people
   Ⓒ 22 people
   Ⓓ 44 people

14. Audrey can watch 5 hours of TV a week. She has already watched 4 shows that are each 1 hour long. How many more hours can she watch TV this week?

   Ⓐ 3 hours
   Ⓑ 2 hours
   Ⓒ 1 hour
   Ⓓ 4 hours

15. Greg had 3 books. His older brother gave him 15 more books. Greg wants to divide his total number of books equally onto 6 shelves. How many books should he place on each shelf?

   Ⓐ 3 books
   Ⓑ 12 books
   Ⓒ 18 books
   Ⓓ 6 books

Name: _____ Date: _____

16. Sarah bought 2 boxes of doughnuts. Each box contained 12 donuts. She shared a total of 7 donuts with her friends. How many doughnuts does she have now? Identify which equations can be used to find the answer. (Choose all correct answers)

   Ⓐ 12 x 2 = 24
   Ⓑ 12 + 2 = 14
   Ⓒ 24 - 7 = 17
   Ⓓ 2 + 12 + 7 = 21

17. Freddy has a collection of 32 baseball cards. He wants to share the cards with 4 classmates. One of the classmates brings 8 more cards to add to the collection. If Freddy and his classmates share all the cards, each receiving the same number, how many cards does each person have? What should be the steps to be followed to arrive at the answer? Write the steps in the correct sequence in the boxes given below.

   Ⓐ 32 - 6 = 26
   Ⓑ 4 + 1 = 5
   Ⓒ 32 + 8 = 40
   Ⓓ 40 ÷ 5 = 8

18. A farmer collected 22 pints of milk from his cows. He put all the milk into bottles. Each bottle holds 2 pints of milk. He accidentally spilled 6 bottles of milk. How many bottles are left with the farmer now? Circle the math sentences that can be used to find the answer. (Circle all correct answers)

   Ⓐ 11
   Ⓑ 24
   Ⓒ 16
   Ⓓ 5

Name: _____ Date: _____

19. For each of the problems in the first column, select the correct answer.

	$50	$5	$10	$4
Karen had 86 dollars. He bought 7 books. After buying them he had 16 dollars. How much did each book cost?	○	○	○	○
Jose and his four friends bought a new board game. It was on sale for 20 dollars off. If each of the boys (total 5 of them) paid $6. What was the original cost of the new board game?	○	○	○	○
A shopkeeper buys 5 pens for $35 and sells them at the rate of $8 per pen. If he sells all the five pens, how much profit he will get?	○	○	○	○
Jeffrey bought 8 actions figures which cost 3 dollars each from John. John bought 6 books from the amount he received from Jeffrey. If the cost of each book John purchased is the same, what is the cost of each book?	○	○	○	○

Online Resources: Two-Step Problems

URL	QR Code
http://lumoslearning.com/a/m13429	

 Videos   Apps   Sample Questions

NOTES

Number Patterns

1. Which of the following is an even number?

    Ⓐ 764,723
    Ⓑ 90,835
    Ⓒ 5,862
    Ⓓ 609

2. Which of these sets contains no odd numbers?

    Ⓐ 13, 15, 81, 109, 199
    Ⓑ 123, 133, 421, 412, 600
    Ⓒ 34, 46, 48, 106, 88
    Ⓓ 12, 37, 6, 14, 144

3. Complete the following statement.
    The sum of two even numbers will always be _____ .

    Ⓐ greater than 10
    Ⓑ less than 100
    Ⓒ even
    Ⓓ odd

4. Complete the following statement.
    The product of two even numbers will always be _____ .

    Ⓐ even
    Ⓑ odd
    Ⓒ a multiple of 10
    Ⓓ a square number

5. Complete the following statement.
    A number has a nine in its ones place. The number must be a multiple of ____.

    Ⓐ 9
    Ⓑ 3
    Ⓒ 7
    Ⓓ None of the above

6. Complete the following statement.
   Numbers that are multiples of 8 are all _____.

   Ⓐ even
   Ⓑ multiples of 2
   Ⓒ multiples of 4
   Ⓓ All of the above

7. If this pattern continues, what will the next 3 numbers be?
   7, 14, 21, 28, 35, ...

   Ⓐ 41, 47, 53
   Ⓑ 49, 56, 63
   Ⓒ 77, 84, 91
   Ⓓ 42, 49, 56

8. Complete the following statement.
   All multiples of _____ can be decomposed into two equal addends.

   Ⓐ 6
   Ⓑ 9
   Ⓒ 3
   Ⓓ 5

9. If this pattern continues, what will the next 3 numbers be?
   9, 18, 27, 36, ...

   Ⓐ 54, 63, 72
   Ⓑ 45, 54, 63
   Ⓒ 44, 52, 60
   Ⓓ 44, 53, 62

10. A number is multiplied by 7 and the resulting product is even. Which of these could have been the number?

    Ⓐ 7
    Ⓑ 17
    Ⓒ 34
    Ⓓ 99

11. Complete the following statement.
    The multiples of 4 will always _____.

    Ⓐ have a 2 in the ones place
    Ⓑ be even
    Ⓒ be divisible by 8
    Ⓓ None of these

12. Complete the following statement.
    The sum of an even number and an odd number will always be _____.

    Ⓐ even
    Ⓑ odd
    Ⓒ divisible by 3
    Ⓓ None of the above

13. Complete the following statement.
    A multiple of 4 can have a _____ in its ones place.

    Ⓐ 2
    Ⓑ 8
    Ⓒ 6
    Ⓓ All of the above

14. Complete the following statement.
    A multiple of 5 can have a _____ as its ones digit.

    Ⓐ 0
    Ⓑ 3
    Ⓒ 9
    Ⓓ All of the above

15. Which of the following would produce an even product?

    Ⓐ an even number times an even number
    Ⓑ an even number times an odd number
    Ⓒ an odd number times an even number
    Ⓓ All of the above

16. Select the number that will come next if the pattern continues.

	10	35	24
2, 4, 6, 8	○	○	○
40, 36, 32, 28	○	○	○
7, 14, 21, 28	○	○	○

17. Type in the numbers that complete the table if the pattern is multiples of 3.

IN	OUT
3	9
4	
5	15
	18
7	

18. If the pattern continues, which of the following numbers will appear?
    Note: More than one option may be correct.

    100, 90, 80, 70

    Ⓐ 50
    Ⓑ 110
    Ⓒ 80
    Ⓓ 60

19. Complete the following statement. If you subtract an odd number from an even number, the difference will always be (a/an) _____. Circle the correct answer.

    Ⓐ Multiple of 3
    Ⓑ Even number
    Ⓒ Odd number
    Ⓓ Odd number or Even number

Name: _____   Date: _____

20. For each statement in the first column, choose all the correct answers.

	2	4	5	7
A number has a four in its ones place. The number can be a multiple of ____.	○	○	○	○
A number has a five in its ones place. The number can be a multiple of ____.	○	○	○	○
A number has a zero in its ones place. The number can be a multiple of ____.	○	○	○	○
A number has a three in its ones place. The number can be a multiple of ____.	○	○	○	○

Online Resources: Number Patterns

URL	QR Code
http://lumoslearning.com/a/m13430	

- Videos
- Apps
- Sample Questions

End of Operations and Algebraic Thinking

NOTES

Answer Key

and

Detailed Explanations

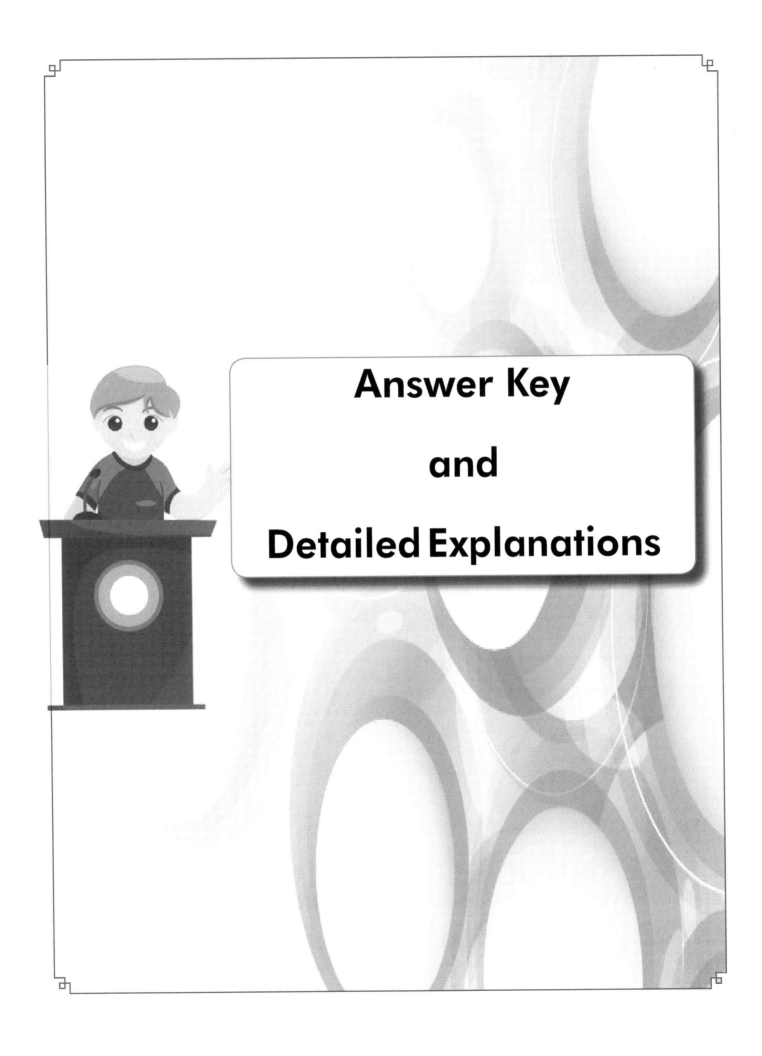

Understanding Multiplication

Question No.	Answer	Detailed Explanation
1	D	The picture depicts 3 sets of 9 objects which is equivalent to 3 x 9 = 27.
2	C	The picture depicts 4 sets of 5 objects which is equivalent to 4 x 5.
3	D	The picture depicts 4 sets of 7 objects which is equivalent to 4 x 7 = 28.
4	A	The picture depicts 2 sets of 12 objects which is equivalent to 2 x 12 = 24.
5	A	The picture depicts 4 sets of 4 objects which is equivalent to 4 x 4 = 16.
6	A	The picture depicts 4 sets of 6 objects which is equivalent to 4 x 6 = 24.
7	D	The picture depicts 3 sets of 6 objects which is equivalent to 6 x 3 (or 3 x 6) = 18
8	D	The picture depicts 5 sets of 3 objects which is equivalent to 3 x 5 (or 5 x 3) = 15.
9	A	The picture depicts 2 sets of 3 objects which is equivalent to 3 x 2 (or 2 x 3) = 6.
10	C	The picture depicts 4 sets of 5 objects which is equivalent to 5 x 4 (or 4 x 5) = 20.
11	B	The picture depicts 4 sets of 2 objects which is equivalent to 4 x 2 = 8.
12	B	The picture depicts 6 sets of 8 objects which is equivalent to 6 x 8 = 48.
13	C	The picture depicts 2 sets of 10 objects which is equivalent to 2 x 10 = 20.
14	A	The picture depicts 5 sets of 5 objects which is equivalent to 5 x 5 = 25.
15	D	The picture depicts 3 sets of 3 objects which is equivalent to 3 x 3 = 9.
16	4x8	The expression 8 + 8 + 8 + 8 has the same value as 4 x 8. Multiplication problems can be solved using repeated addition. Adding 4 groups of 8 is the same as multiplying 4 groups of 8.

17.

	Column A: 3+3+3+3+3+3	Column B: 3+3+3+3+3+3+3+3	Column C: 3+3+3
3 x 8	○	●	○
3 x 3	○	○	●
3 x 6	●	○	○

Question No.	Answer	Detailed Explanation
18	2x5 3x6 2x4	2 groups of 5 objects represents the expression 2 x 5. 3 groups of 6 objects represents the expression 3 x 6. 2 groups of 4 objects represents the expression 2 x 4.
19 A		Yes, John is correct. 8 x 6 = 8 x (5 + 1). Then John used the distributive property. 8 x (5 + 1) = 8 x 5 + 8 x 1 = 8 x 5 + 8.
19 B		Let n be the total number of pens the boys buy all together. n = (number of pens each boy buys) x (number of boys) = 6 x 7 = 42 pens
20		Number of lions: 5, 6, 9, 8, 4 Total number of legs: 20, 24, 36, 32, 16

Understanding Division

Question No.	Answer	Detailed Explanation
1	D	There are 100 items that need to be divided into 10 groups. 100 ÷ 10 = 10.
2	C	There are 15 items that need to be divided into 3 groups. 15 ÷ 3 = 5.
3	A	There are 50 items that need to be divided into 5 groups. 50 ÷ 5 = 10.
4	D	There are 30 items that need to be sorted into 6 groups. 30 ÷ 6 = 5.
5	B	There are 80 items that need to be sorted into groups of 10. 80 ÷ 10 = 8.
6	B	There are 15 items that need to be shared with 5 groups. 15 ÷ 5 = 3.
7	D	There are 81 items that need to be divided into 9 groups. 81 ÷ 9 = 9.
8	C	There are 40 items that need to be sorted into groups of 10. 40 ÷ 10 = 4.
9	B	There are 20 items that need to be sorted into groups of 5. 20 ÷ 5 = 4.
10	A	There are 30 people who need to be divided into 5 groups. 30 ÷ 5 = 6.
11	D	There are 24 items that need to be sorted into groups of 3. 24 ÷ 3 = 8.
12	B	There are 44 items that need to be divided into 4 groups. 44 ÷ 4 = 11.
13	C	All together, the group has 32 + 4 marbles which equals 36. There are 4 people in the group. There are 36 items that need to be shared with 4 groups. 36 ÷ 4 = 9.
14	B	There are 100 items (dollars) that need to be divided into 5 groups. $100 ÷ 5 = $20.
15	D	There are 26 items that need to be shared equally between two people. 26 ÷ 2 = 13.
16	4 slices	There is a total of 8 slices to be divided among 2 people. 8 ÷ 2 = 4.
17	A & C	The correct answers are A and C. There is a total of 16 stickers to be divided into equal groups. The stickers can be divided into 2 equal groups of 8. The stickers can also be divided into 4 equal groups of 4.
18	A	Picture A represents the expression 10 ÷ 5. In the picture, there is a total of 10 objects divided into 5 equal groups.

Question No.	Answer	Detailed Explanation		
19	5; 10; 50	**Dividend**		**Possible Divisors**	
		100		2	
		100		4	
		100		**5**	
		100		**10**	
		100		20	
		100		25	
		100		**50**	
20			<	>	=
		30 ÷ 5 ___ 42 ÷ 6	●	○	○
		72 ÷ 8 ___ 63 ÷ 7	○	○	●
		54 ÷ 6 ___ 56 ÷ 7	○	●	○

Applying Multiplication & Division

Question No.	Answer	Detailed Explanation
1	B	Product refers to the result of the multiplication of two or more numbers. 54 and 3 are both factors.
2	D	The phrase "twice as many" indicates that if a number is multiplied by 2, the product will reflect two times, or twice, the original amount. In this case, the product of 30 popcorn balls is already known. The product must be then divided by 2 in order to find the number of cotton candies. 30÷2=15.
3	C	The phrase "8 times as many" indicates that if Sue's amount of DVDs is multiplied by 8, the product will be equal to the amount of Monica's DVDs. To solve for Sue use the equation n x 8 = 56. When trying to solve for a missing number in a multiplication equation, you must divide the product by the given number. 56÷8=7
4	A	Marcus' jumping jack is equivalent to 4 times that of Jonathan. 7 x 4= 28.
5	D	Marsha's movie count is equivalent to 3 times that of Jonathan's. 3 x 4= 12.
6	B	There are 4 groups and each group has 9 items. This indicates that if the number of groups is multiplied by the number of items in each group, the product will reflect the total number of items in all. 4 x 9= 36.
7	B	The number of students can be divided by the number of slices in each pizza. The quotient will reflect the number of pizzas needed. 24 ÷ 12 = 2 pizzas.
8	C	The total number of apples can be divided by the number of apples needed for each pie. The quotient will reflect the number of pies that can be made. 27 ÷ 3= 9.
9	C	The number of rows multiplied by the number of seeds in each row must equal 48. All answer choices given contain two numbers with a product of 48 except Option C. 7 x 7 = 49.
10	B	The total number of students can be divided by the number of teams. The quotient will reflect the number of students on each team. 25 ÷ 5= 5.
11	A	The number of chapters can be divided by the number of days. The quotient will reflect the number of chapters that can be read each day. 21 ÷ 7 = 3.

Question No.	Answer	Detailed Explanation
12	D	The $40 Devon has can be divided by the cost of one gallon of fuel ($5). The quotient will reflect the number of gallons Devon can afford to buy. $40 ÷ $5 = 8 gallons.
13	B	There are 4 cups needed for one batch. Amanda is making 3 batches, so she needs 4 sets of 3 cups or 4 x 3 = 12 cups.
14	C	The phrase "twice as many" indicates that if a number is multiplied by 2 the product will reflect two times, or twice, the original amount. The amount of friends invited (20) must be multiplied by 2 in order to find out how many friends attended. The correct number sentence is 20 x 2 = 40.
15	C	Product refers to multiplication. The problem states that 9 and a number (n) when multiplied together equals 45. The correct number sentence is 9 x n = 45.
16	B & C	The correct number sentences are 5 x 6= 30 and 6 x 5= 30. There are 5 groups of 6 desks. In order to find the total number of desks, multiply 5 by 6. The rule of communicative property states that 5 x 6=6 x 5. Therefore 6 x 5= 30 is correct as well.
17	C	Each friend should receive 6 flowers. There are 24 flowers to be divided among 4 people. In order to find the number of flowers per person, divide 24 by 4. 24 ÷ 4= 6.
18	8	This is a problem on division. Number of cupcakes each boy gets = Total number of cupcakes ÷ number of boys= 48 ÷ 6 = 8 cupcakes
19 Part A	x	First, we find the value of 64 ÷ 8. 64 ÷ 8 = 8. Now, we have to find the correct symbol to make the equation 8 = 2 ___ 4, true. Multiplying 2 by 4, we get 8. Therefore, x (multiplication symbol) is the correct choice.
19 Part B	+	First, we find the value of 42 ÷ 7. 42 ÷ 7 = 6. Now, we have to find the correct symbol to make the equation 2 ___ 4 = 6, true. If we add 2 and 4, we get 6. Therefore, + (plus) is the correct choice.
20		Let n be the number of days Joseph takes to complete the book, p be the number of pages in the book (p = 56) and r be the number of pages he reads every day (r = 8). n = p ÷ r = 56 ÷ 8 = 7 days

Finding Unknown Values

Question No.	Answer	Detailed Explanation
1	C	To solve for an unknown in a multiplication problem, you must do the opposite operation, which is to divide. You must divide the product by the given factor. 30 ÷ 6=5. n = 5.
2	A	To solve for an unknown in a multiplication problem, you must do the opposite operation, which is to divide. You must divide the product by the given factor. 21 ÷ 7=3. The missing value is 3.
3	A	To solve for an unknown in a multiplication problem, you must do the opposite operation, which is to divide. You must divide the product by the given factor. 36 ÷ 4= 9. The missing value is 9.
4	C	The first step to solve for an unknown in a division problem is to decide which part of the problem is missing: Dividend: n Divisor: 9 Quotient: 8 When solving for the dividend, you must multiply the divisor and the quotient. 9 x 8 = 72. n = 72.
5	B	The first step to solve for an unknown in a division problem is to decide which part of the problem is missing: Dividend: n Divisor: 3 Quotient: 10 When solving for the dividend, you must multiply the divisor and the quotient. 3 x 10 = 30. n = 30.
6	C	The first step to solve for an unknown in a division problem is to decide which part of the problem is missing: Dividend: 45 Divisor: n Quotient: 9 When solving for the divisor, you must divide the dividend by the quotient. 45 ÷ 9 = 5.
7	C	To solve for an unknown in a multiplication problem, you must do the opposite operation, which is to divide. You must divide the product by the given factor. 64 ÷ 8 = 8. n = 8.

Question No.	Answer	Detailed Explanation
8	B	The first step to solve for an unknown in a division problem is to decide which part of the problem is missing: Dividend: 12 Divisor: (?) Quotient: 2 When solving for the divisor, you must divide the dividend by the quotient. 12 ÷ 2 = 6. The unknown value is 6.
9	C	The first step to solve for an unknown in a division problem is to decide which part of the problem is missing: Dividend: (?) Divisor: 7 Quotient: 11 When solving for the dividend, you must multiply the divisor and the quotient. 7 x 11 = 77. The missing value is 77.
10	B	To solve for an unknown in a multiplication problem, you must do the opposite operation, which is to divide. You must divide the product by the given factor. 16 ÷ 4 = 4. n = 4.
11	B	To solve for an unknown in a multiplication problem, you must do the opposite operation, which is to divide. You must divide the product by the given factor. 56 ÷ 7 = 8. m = 8.
12	B	The first step to solve for an unknown in a division problem is to decide which part of the problem is missing: Dividend: 60 Divisor: n Quotient: 5 When solving for the divisor, you must divide the dividend by the quotient. 60 ÷ 5 = 12. The unknown value is 12.
13	B	To solve for an unknown in a multiplication problem, you must do the opposite operation, which is to divide. You must divide the product by the given factor. 81 ÷ 9 = 9. z = 9.
14	C	The first step to solve for an unknown in a division problem is to decide which part of the problem is missing: Dividend: n Divisor: 3 Quotient: 3 When solving for the dividend, you must multiply the divisor and the quotient. 3 x 3 = 9. p = 9.

Question No.	Answer	Detailed Explanation
15	A	The first step to solve for an unknown in a division problem is to decide which part of the problem is missing: Dividend: 10 Divisor: n Quotient: 10 When solving for the divisor, you must divide the dividend by the quotient. 10 ÷ 10 = 1. n = 1.
16	54	54 items divided into 6 groups will contain 9 items in each group. 54 ÷ 6= 9.
17	B & D	7 groups of 2 items is a total of 14 items. 7 x 2= 14.
18	32; 9; 15 and 7	<table><tr><th>Equation</th><th>Product</th></tr><tr><td>4 x 8=</td><td>32</td></tr><tr><td>9</td><td>x 7 = 63</td></tr><tr><td>3 x 5=</td><td>15</td></tr><tr><td>7</td><td>x 1 =7</td></tr></table>
19 Part A		Let **t** be the cost of 6 pens, **c** be the cost of 1 pen (c = $7) and **n** be the number of pens (n = 6). t = c x n
19 Part B		We know that t=c x n, substituting the values, we get: t= 7 x 6 t= $42
20		<table><tr><th>Equation</th><th>n=7</th><th>n=6</th></tr><tr><td>3 × 8 = 4 × n</td><td>○</td><td>●</td></tr><tr><td>72 ÷ 9 = 56 ÷ n</td><td>●</td><td>○</td></tr></table>

Multiplication & Division Properties

Question No.	Answer	Detailed Explanation
1	D	In order for the statement to be true, the answer on both sides of the equal sign must be the same. All of the answer choices are equal except for the last choice. 12 x 1 = 12 and 12 x 12 = 144. 12 x 1 is not equal to 12 x 12.
2	A	Option A is the only one that is true because 11 x 6 = 66 and 6 x 11 = 66. This is an example of the Commutative Property of Multiplication.
3	C	In multiplication, the only time that the number 0 will be the product is when at least one of the factors is 0. Option C is the only choice that fits this rule.
4	C	In multiplication, the only time that the number 0 will be the product is when at least one of the factors is 0. In division, the only time that the number 0 will be the answer is when the dividend is 0. Option C is the only choice where the equation fits this rule.
5	C	The Identity Property of Multiplication states that any number multiplied by 1 equals itself.
6	A	The Commutative Property of Multiplication states that the order of the factors does not change the answer.
7	B	The Associative Property of Multiplication states that the grouping of factors does not change the answer.
8	D	The Distributive Property states that multiplying a number by a group of numbers added together is the same as doing each multiplication problem separately.
9	C	The Commutative Property of Multiplication states that the order of the factors does not change the answer. 4 x 5 = 20 is the same as 5 x 4 = 20.
10	A	The Associative Property of Multiplication states that the grouping of factors does not change the answer. So (2 x 3) x 4 = 24 is the same as 2 x (3 x 4) = 24.
11	C	Inverse operations mean that one operation will reverse the effect of another. Division is the inverse of multiplication and vice versa. For example, if 4 x 3 = 12 then 12 ÷ 3 = 4 and 12 ÷ 4 = 3.
12	A	The Commutative Property of Multiplication states that the order of the factors does not change the answer.
13	D	The Distributive Property states that multiplying a number by a group of numbers added together is the same as doing each multiplication separately.
14	C	The Identity Property of Multiplication states that any number multiplied by 1 equals itself.

Question No.	Answer	Detailed Explanation
15	A	The Identity Property of Multiplication states that any number multiplied by 1 equals itself. 10 x 1 = 10.
16	C & D	Commutative property is the rule that states a x b = b x a. According to this rule, 4 x 5 = 5 x 4.
17	1	Identity property is the rule that states that when a number is multiplied by 1, the product, is the original number. This applies to the equation 7 x 1= 7.
18	A	Associative property is the rule that states that when the grouping of factors changes, the product remains the same. This applies to the equations (2 x 3) x 4 = 24 and 2 x (3 x 4) = 24.
19 Part A	3	The commutative property of multiplication states that the order of the factors does not change the answer. Here, 3 and 7 are the factors on the left side. Therefore, the unknown factor on the right side has to be 3.
19 Part B	Commutative property	The answer is commutative property. The property states that a x b = b x a.
20		

	3 x (5 x 7) = (3 x 5) x 7	3 x 1 = 3	3 x 5 = 5 x 3	3 x (5 + 7) = (3 x 5) + (3 x 7)
Commutative Property	○	○	●	○
Associative Property	●	○	○	○
Identity Property	○	●	○	○
Distributive Property	○	○	○	●

Relating Multiplication & Division

Question No.	Answer	Detailed Explanation
1	B	5 x 6 = 30 is equivalent to 30 ÷ 6 = 5 because 5 groups of 6 objects is equivalent to 30.
2	C	7 x 3 = 21 is equivalent to 21 ÷ 3 = 7 because 7 groups of 3 objects is equivalent to 21.
3	B	8 x 9 = 72 is equivalent to 72 ÷ 9 = 8 because 8 groups of 9 objects is equivalent to 72.
4	D	10 x 5 = 50 is equivalent to 50 ÷ 10 = 5 because 10 groups of 5 objects is equivalent to 50.
5	A	4 x 9 = 36 is equivalent to 36 ÷ 4 = 9 because 4 groups of 9 objects is equivalent to 36.
6	B & C	Since there are 9 students who need 5 sheets each, this is equivalent to 9 x 5 which equals 45, or 45 ÷ 5 = 9.
7	B	Since there are 8 touchdowns each worth 7 points, this is equivalent to 8 x 7 which equals 56, or 56 ÷ 7 = 8.
8	C	There are 12 items in a pack and there are 96 items needed. To see how many packs are needed, you must divide 96 ÷ 12 = 8, or 8 x 12 = 96.
9	B	There are 12 tables and 84 students which means there are 84 students who need to be divided into groups of 12, which is 84 ÷ 12 = 7 or 12 x 7 = 84.
10	D	There are 8 people, Walter plus his 7 friends who need to evenly split 16 slices of pizza which is equivalent to 16 ÷ 8 = 2, or 8 x 2 = 16.
11	C	Equations in a fact family utilize the same numbers in a multiplication or division problem and are equivalent. 6 x 5 = 30 is equivalent to 30 ÷ 5 = 6.
12	C	Multiplication and division are inverse operations. This means that when two numbers are multiplied, the product can be divided by either of the two factors to give the other factor. 4 x n = 32 is equivalent to 32 ÷ 4 = n
13	D	Multiplication and division are inverse operations. This means that when two numbers are multiplied, the product can be divided by either of the two factors to give the other factor. n x 6 = 48 is equivalent to 48 ÷ n = 6
14	C	Multiplication and division are inverse operations. This means that when two numbers are multiplied, the product can be divided by either of the two factors to give the other factor. 45 ÷ n = 9 is equivalent to 9 x n = 45.

Question No.	Answer	Detailed Explanation
15	B	There are 32 items that need to be evenly split into 2 groups which is equivalent to 32 ÷ 2 = 16, or 16 x 2 = 32.
16		See table below

	40÷5=8	36÷6=6	21÷7=3	18÷9=2
6 x 6= 36	○	●	○	○
9 x 2= 18	○	○	○	●
5 x 8= 40	●	○	○	○
7 x 3= 21	○	○	●	○

Question No.	Answer	Detailed Explanation
17	4; 7 and 27	See table below

	Division Expression	Quotient
If 4 x 4= 16 then...	16 ÷ 4=	**4**
If 7 x 6= 42 then... 42 ÷	**7**	6
If 3 x 9= 27 then...	**27**	÷ 3=9

Question No.	Answer	Detailed Explanation
18	B & C	Multiplication and division can be related to one another in the sense that if a x b= c then c ÷ b= a or c ÷ a= b. Therefore, both 7 x 9= 63 and 9 x 7= 63 relate to 63 ÷ 9= 7.
19	A	Multiplication and division are inverse operations. This means that when two numbers are multiplied, the product we get can be divided by either of the two factors to give the other factor. Here, the product (65) is divided by one of the factors (n) to get the other factor (5). Therefore, the equivalent number sentence is 65 = 5 x n. Note that 5 x n can also be written as n x 5 (commutative property).
20 Part A	>	40 ÷ 5 > 54 ÷ 9
20 Part B	<	35 ÷ 7 < 28 ÷ 4
20 Part C	=	18 ÷ 6 = 24 ÷ 8

Multiplication & Division Facts

Question No.	Answer	Detailed Explanation
1	C	In multiplication, if one of the factors is 0, the product is also 0.
2	C	The Identity Property of Multiplication states that any number multiplied by 1 equals itself, number so 1 x 10 = 10.
3	A	3 x 8 represents 3 groups of 8 items. There are 24 items in total.
4	B	5 x 9 represents 5 groups of 9 items. There are 45 items in total
5	C	Product refers to the answer when numbers are multiplied. 8 x 6 represents 8 groups of 6 items. There are 48 items in total.
6	C	Product refers to the answer when numbers are multiplied. 7 x 7 represents 7 groups of 7 items. There are 49 items in total.
7	B	Product refers to the answer when numbers are multiplied. 4 x 6 represents 4 groups of 6 items. There are 24 items in total.
8	A	Product refers to the answer when numbers are multiplied. 6 x 9 represents 6 groups of 9 items. There are 54 items in total.
9	B	Product refers to the answer when numbers are multiplied. 9 x 8 represents 9 groups of 8 items. There are 72 items in total.
10	D	Product refers to the answer when numbers are multiplied. Option D is the only choice in which the answer is 48.
11	B	The quotient refers to the answer when a number is divided by another number. There are 25 items that need to be divided into 5 groups. 25 ÷ 5 = 5.
12	B	There are 32 items that need to be divided into 4 groups. 32 ÷ 4 = 8
13	A	There are 28 items that need to be divided into 7 groups. 28 ÷ 7 = 4. The quotient refers to the answer when a number is divided by another number.
14	A	When the number 0 is divided by any non-zero number, the answer is always 0. The quotient refers to the answer when a number is divided by another number.
15	C	When a number is divided by 1, the answer is always the original number.
16	D	The quotient refers to the answer when a number is divided by another number. There are 12 items that need to be divided into 2 groups. 12 ÷ 2 = 6.
17	B	There are 63 items that need to be divided into 9 groups. 63 ÷ 9 = 7.

Question No.	Answer	Detailed Explanation
18	B	There are 42 items that need to be divided into 7 groups. 42 ÷ 7 = 6
19	A	The quotient refers to the answer when a number is divided by another number. There are 33 items that need to be divided into 3 groups. 33 ÷ 3 = 11.
20	C	There are 56 items that need to be divided into 7 groups. 56 ÷ 7 = 8.
21	B	4 x 12 represents 4 groups of 12 items. There are 48 items total.
22	B	There are 75 items that need to be divided into 5 groups. 75 ÷ 5 = 15
23	A	There are 84 items that need to be divided into 12 groups. 84 ÷ 12 = 7.
24	B	12 x 3 represents 12 groups of 3 items. There are 36 items total.
25	B	There are 36 items that need to be divided into 3 groups. 36 ÷ 3 = 12.
26	C	There are 60 items that need to be divided into 5 groups. 60 ÷ 5 = 12.
27	B	11 x 4 represents 11 groups of 4 items. There are 44 items total.
28	A	There are 80 items that need to be divided into 8 groups. 80 ÷ 8 = 10.
29	D	12 x 8 represents 12 groups of 8 items. There are 96 items total.
30	C	There are 50 items that need to be divided into 5 groups. 50 ÷ 5 = 10.

31

	12	18	32
6 x 3=	○	●	○
8 x 4=	○	○	●
4 x 3=	●	○	○
9 x 2=	○	●	○

Question No.	Answer	Detailed Explanation
32	6	The quotient is the result of dividing a number by another number. The quotient of 24 ÷ 4 is 6.
33	A & D	Product refers to the answer when numbers are multiplied. 6 x 6 = 36 and 9 x 4 = 36. Therefore, options (A) and (D) are correct.
34	C	The quotient refers to the answer when a number is divided by another number. There are 27 items that need to be divided into 9 groups. 27 ÷ 9 = 3.

35

5	x	8		=	
8	÷		=	8
	÷	7	=	0
6	x		=	30

Two-Step Problems

Question No.	Answer	Detailed Explanation
1	C	First, calculate how many cards Danny has by subtracting 11 from 47; 47 - 11 = 36. Then divide this number by 3 to see how many each classmate will receive; 36 ÷ 3 = 12.
2	C	First, calculate how many students are in each class. The first class has 3 rows of 7 students and 3 x 7 = 21. The second class has 4 rows of 5 students and 4 x 5 = 20. Then add both totals to calculate the total number of students outside; 21 + 20 = 41.
3	D	First, calculate how much more money Jessica needs to save by subtracting what she has from what she needs; $100 - $60 = $40. Jessica needs 40 more dollars. Now divide 40 dollars by the amount she makes each hour of babysitting to find how many more hours she needs to work to earn the rest of the money; $40 ÷ 10 = 4.
4	A	First calculate how many cookies George began with by multiplying 2 and 10; 2 x 10 = 20. Then subtract the number of cookies he gave to his parents from this total; 20 - 12 = 8.
5	A	First calculate the total number of minutes Renae spends doing chores by multiplying 3 and 15; 3 x 15 = 45. Then subtract this number from 60 minutes to see how many minutes she has remaining to do her homework; 60 - 45 = 15.
6	C	First calculate the sale price of the game; $28 - 4 = $24. Then divide this answer by 2 to see how much each girl will pay; $24 ÷ 2 = $12.
7	B	First, calculate how many students rode the bus by subtracting the number of students who rode in cars from the total number of students; 100 - 10 = 90. Then divide this answer by the number of buses to see how many students rode on each bus; 90 ÷ 5 = 18.
8	D	First, calculate the number of books the sister has by multiplying the number of books Julia has by 2; 32 x 2 = 64. Then add this number to Julia's amount to get the total books; 64 + 32 = 96.
9	B	First, calculate the total number of apples Alicia has by multiplying 5 and 8; 5 x 8 = 40. Then calculate the number of apples in each bag by dividing the total number of apples by the number of bags; 40 ÷ 10 = 4.
10	A	First, subtract the cost of the markers from the total amount spent; $19 - 4 = $15. Then divide this answer by the number of books bought to calculate the cost of each book; $15 ÷ 3 = $5.

Question No.	Answer	Detailed Explanation
11	C	First, calculate how many candy bars were given to friends by multiplying the total number of friends by the number of bars each friend received; 7 x 2 = 14. Then subtract this answer from the total number of candy bars Brian won; 24 - 14 = 10.
12	A	First, calculate how many mini cupcakes were given to the sisters by multiplying the total number of sisters by the number each one received; 3 x 3 = 9. Then add this number to the number of cupcakes Jenine had left for herself; 9 + 4 = 13.
13	B	First, calculate how many people visited the museum on Saturday by multiplying the number of Friday visitors by 2 (for twice as many); 22 x 2 = 44. Then add this number to the number of Friday visitors; 44 + 22 = 66.
14	C	First, calculate how many hours Audrey has already watched TV by multiplying the number of shows she has watched by the length of each show; 4 x 1 = 4. Then subtract this answer from the total number of hours she is allowed to watch; 5 - 4 = 1.
15	A	First, calculate the total number of books Greg has by adding the number of books given to him by his brother to the number of books he already had; 15 + 3 = 18. Then calculate the number of books on each shelf by dividing the total number of books by the number of shelves; 18 ÷ 6 = 3.
16	A & C	There are two steps required to find the answer. First, in order to figure out the total of doughnuts multiply 2 boxes by 12 doughnuts. 12 x 2= 24. Then subtract the amount of donuts Sarah shared with friends. 24-7= 17.
17	1. C 2. B 3. D	There are three steps required to find the answer. First, in order to figure out the total amount of baseball cards, add Freddy's 32 cards to his classmate's 8 cards. 32 + 8= 40. Then to figure out the total amount of people, add Freddy to his 4 classmates. 4 + 1= 5. The last step is to divide the total amount of cards among 5 people. 40 ÷ 5= 8.
18	D	First step is total number of bottles the farmer needed: 22 ÷ 2 = 11. Next step: Number of bottles left after he spilled 6 bottles: 11 - 6 = 5. So, Option (D) is to be circled.

Question No.	Answer		Detailed Explanation			
19			$50	$5	$10	$4
	Karen had 86 dollars. He bought 7 books. After buying them he had 16 dollars. How much did each book cost?		○	○	●	○
	Jose and his four friends bought a new board game. It was on sale for 20 dollars off. If each of the boys (total 5 of them) paid $6. What was the original cost of the new board game?		●	○	○	○
	A shopkeeper buys 5 pens for $35 and sells them at the rate of $8 per pen. If he sells all the five pens, how much profit he will get?		○	●	○	○
	Jeffrey bought 8 actions figures which cost 3 dollars each from John. John bought 6 books from the amount he received from Jeffrey. If the cost of each book John purchased is the same, what is the cost of each book?		○	○	○	●

Solution to problem 1 : First, subtract $16 from $86 to get the cost of 7 books; 86 - 16 = $70. Then divide $70 by 7 to get the cost of one book. Cost of one book = 70 ÷ 7 = $10.

Solution to problem 2 : First, multiply 5 by $6 to get the total amount paid by the boys; 5 x 6 = $30. Then add $20 to $30 to get the original cost of the new board game; 20 + 30 = $50.

Solution to problem 3 : First, multiply 5 by 8 to calculate the total amount of money the shopkeeper gets; 5 x 8 = $40. Then subtract $35 from $40 to get the profit he earns; 40 - 35 = $5.

Solution to problem 4 : First, multiply 8 by $3 to get the amount received by John; 8 x 3 = $24. Then divide $24 by 6 to get the cost of each book; 24 ÷ 6 = $4.

Number Patterns

Question No.	Answer	Detailed Explanation
1	C	An even number is any number whose ones digit is one of the following numbers: 0, 2, 4, 6, 8. Option C is the only choice that fits this criteria.
2	C	An odd number is any number whose ones digit is one of the following numbers: 1, 3, 5, 7, 9. Option C is the only choice that does not contain any numbers that fit this criteria.
3	C	The rule states that when two even numbers are added, the answer will always be even. For example, 34 + 12 = 46.
4	A	The rule states that when two even numbers are multiplied, the product will always be even. For example, 34 x 4 = 136.
5	D	There is not enough information given for us to decide if the number is a multiple of 3, 7, or 9. For example, if the original number was 19, it would not be a multiple of 3, 7, or 9.
6	D	Any multiple of an even number is also even. Numbers that are multiples of 8 are also multiples of 2 and 4 because 2 and 4 are factors of 8.
7	D	The pattern is adding 7 to each number to make the next number (7 + 7 = 14, 14 + 7 = 21 and so on). The next number will be 35 + 7 = 42, the next will be 42 + 7 = 49, and the next will be 49 + 7 = 56. These numbers also represent the multiples of 7 in order.
8	A	"Two equal addends" means the number can be divided into two equal numbers. This can be performed on all even numbers. The number 6 is an even number and all of its multiples are also even.
9	B	The pattern is adding 9 to each number to make the next number (9 + 9 = 18, 18 + 9 = 27 and so on). The next number will be 36 + 9 = 45, the next will be 45 + 9 = 54, and the next will be 54 + 9 = 63.
10	C	If an odd number is multiplied by an even number, the answer will be an even number.
11	B	Multiples of even numbers are always even. Four is an even number, so all of its multiples are also even.
12	B	The rule states that when an odd number is added to an even number, the answer will always be odd. For example, 45 + 18 = 63.
13	D	The multiples of 4 are {4, 8, 12, 16, 20, 24, 28, 32, . . .} It is apparent from this list that a multiple of 4 could have a 6, 8, or 2 as its ones digit.
14	A	All multiples of 5 have a number 0 or 5 in the ones position. For example, 205 and 210 are both multiples of 5.
15	D	Whenever an even number is multiplied by any number, the answer will always be even.

Question No.	Answer	Detailed Explanation
16	(see table)	If the pattern in the first row continues to increase by 2, the next number will be 10. If the pattern in the second row continues to decrease by 4, the next number will be 24. If the pattern in the last row continues to increase by 7, the next number will be 35.

	10	35	24
2, 4, 6, 8	●	○	○
40, 36, 32, 28	○	○	●
7, 14, 21, 28	○	●	○

Question No.	Answer	Detailed Explanation
17	12; 6; 21; 8; 24	If the pattern continues to increase by multiples of 3, the missing numbers will be 12, 6, 21, 8 and 24.

IN	OUT
3	9
4	**12**
5	15
6	18
7	**21**
8	**24**

Question No.	Answer	Detailed Explanation
18	A & D	If the pattern continues to decrease by 10, the only numbers that will appear from the answer choices are 50 and 60.
19	C	When you add two odd numbers, the sum is an even number. Addition and subtraction are inverse operations. Therefore, when you subtract an odd number from an even number, the difference has to be an odd number. If a and b are odd numbers, the sum (c = a + b) is an even number. Therefore, c - a (= b) or c - b (= a) has to be an odd number.
20	(see table)	

	2	4	5	7
A number has a four in its ones place. The number can be a multiple of ____.	●	●	○	●
A number has a five in its ones place. The number can be a multiple of ____.	○	○	●	●
A number has a zero in its ones place. The number can be a multiple of ____.	●	●	●	●
A number has a three in its ones place. The number can be a multiple of ____.	○	○	○	●

Statement 1: A multiple of 5 cannot have four in the ones place. A multiple of 2 or 4 or 7 can have four in the ones place. For ex. 2 x 2 = 4, 4 x 6 = 24, 2 x 7 = 14.
Statement 2: A multiple of 2 or 4 cannot have five in the ones place. A multiple of 5 or 7 can have five in the ones place. For ex. 5 x 7 = 35.
Statement 3: Any number when multiplied by 10 results in a number with a zero in the ones place. For ex. 2 x 10 = 20, 4 x 10 = 40, 5 x 10 = 50, 7 x 10 = 70.
Statement 4: Multiples of 2, or 4, or 5 cannot have three in the ones place. A multiple of 7 can have 3 in the ones place. For ex. 7 x 9 = 63.

NOTES

Additional Information

What if I buy more than one Lumos Study Program?

Step 1 — Visit the URL and login to your account.
http://www.lumoslearning.com

Step 2 — Click on 'My tedBooks' under the "Account" tab. Place the Book Access Code and submit.

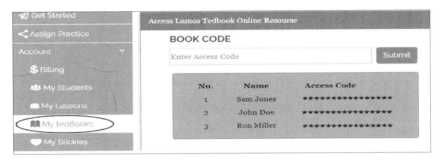

Step 3 — To add the new book for a registered student, choose the ⊙ Existing Student button and select the student and submit.

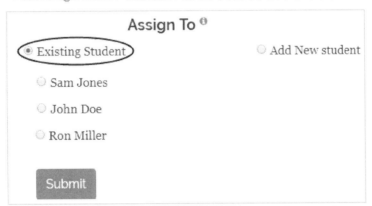

To add the new book for a new student, choose the ⊙ Add New student button and complete the student registration.

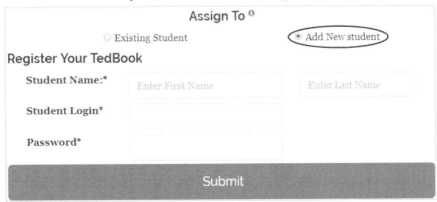

Lumos StepUp® Mobile App FAQ For Students

What is the Lumos StepUp® App?

It is a FREE application you can download onto your Android Smartphones, tablets, iPhones, and iPads.

What are the Benefits of the StepUp® App?

This mobile application gives convenient access to Practice Tests, Common Core State Standards, Online Workbooks, and learning resources through your Smartphone and tablet computers.

- Eleven Technology enhanced question types in both MATH and ELA
- Sample questions for Arithmetic drills
- Standard specific sample questions
- Instant access to the Common Core State Standards
- Jokes and cartoons to make learning fun!

Do I Need the StepUp® App to Access Online Workbooks?

No, you can access Lumos StepUp® Online Workbooks through a personal computer. The StepUp® app simply enhances your learning experience and allows you to conveniently access StepUp® Online Workbooks and additional resources through your smart phone or tablet.

How can I Download the App?

Visit **lumoslearning.com/a/stepup-app** using your Smartphone or tablet and follow the instructions to download the app.

QR Code
for Smartphone
Or Tablet Users

Lumos StepUp® Mobile App FAQ
For Parents and Teachers

What is the Lumos StepUp® App?
It is a free app that teachers can use to easily access real-time student activity information as well as assign learning resources to students. Parents can also use it to easily access school-related information such as homework assigned by teachers and PTA meetings. It can be downloaded onto smart phones and tablets from popular App Stores.

What are the Benefits of the Lumos StepUp® App?
It provides convenient access to

- Standards aligned learning resources for your students
- An easy to use Dashboard
- Student progress reports
- Active and inactive students in your classroom
- Professional development information
- Educational Blogs

How can I Download the App?
Visit **lumoslearning.com/a/stepup-app** using your Smartphone or tablet and follow the instructions to download the app.

QR Code
for Smartphone
Or Tablet Users

Common Core Standards Cross-reference Table

CCSS	Standard Description	Page No.	Question No.
3.OA.A.1	Interpret products of whole numbers, e.g., interpret 5 × 7 as the total number of objects in 5 groups of 7 objects each. For example, describe a context in which a total number of objects can be expressed as 5 × 7.	4	1 to 20
3.OA.A.2	Interpret whole-number quotients of whole numbers, e.g., interpret 56 ÷ 8 as the number of objects in each share when 56 objects are partitioned equally into 8 shares, or as a number of shares when 56 objects are partitioned into equal shares of 8 objects each. For example, describe a context in which a number of shares or a number of groups can be expressed as 56 ÷ 8.	14	1 to 20
3.OA.A.3	Use multiplication and division within 100 to solve word problems in situations involving equal groups, arrays, and measurement quantities, e.g., by using drawings and equations with a symbol for the unknown number to represent the problem.	20	1 to 20
3.OA.A.4	Determine the unknown whole number in a multiplication or division equation relating three whole numbers. For example, determine the unknown number that makes the equation true in each of the equations 8 × ? = 48, 5 = _ ÷ 3, 6 × 6 = ?	26	1 to 20
3.OA.B.5	Apply properties of operations as strategies to multiply and divide.[2] Examples: If 6 × 4 = 24 is known, then 4 × 6 = 24 is also known. (Commutative property of multiplication.) 3 × 5 × 2 can be found by 3 × 5 = 15, then 15 × 2 = 30, or by 5 × 2 = 10, then 3 × 10 = 30. (Associative property of multiplication.) Knowing that 8 × 5 = 40 and 8 × 2 = 16, one can find 8 × 7 as 8 × (5 + 2) = (8 × 5) + (8 × 2) = 40 + 16 = 56. (Distributive property.)	32	1 to 20
3.OA.B.6	Understand division as an unknown-factor problem. For example, find 32 ÷ 8 by finding the number that makes 32 when multiplied by 8.	38	1 to 20
3.OA.C.7	Fluently multiply and divide within 100, using strategies such as the relationship between multiplication and division (e.g., knowing that 8 × 5 = 40, one knows 40 ÷ 5 = 8) or properties of operations. By the end of Grade 3, know from memory all products of two one-digit numbers.	45	1 to 35

CCSS	Standard Description	Page No.	Question No.
3.OA.D.8	Solve two-step word problems using the four operations. Represent these problems using equations with a letter standing for the unknown quantity. Assess the reasonableness of answers using mental computation and estimation strategies including rounding.	53	1 to 19
3.OA.D.9	Identify arithmetic patterns (including patterns in the addition table or multiplication table), and explain them using properties of operations. For example, observe that 4 times a number is always even, and explain why 4 times a number can be decomposed into two equal addends.	59	1 to 20

 # Test Prep and Smart Homework Help

Lumos StepUp is a unique e-Learning program that provides online resources along with personalized coaching to help improve student achievement.

 Practice Assessments that mirror standardized Tests

 Parent Portal: Review online work of your child

 Individualized homework assistance (StepUp® Coach™)

 Student Portal: Anywhere access to Learning Resources

15 Master Tech Enhanced Question Types

 Discover Educational Apps, Books, and Videos

 888-309-8227

 www.lumoslearning.com/stepup

School Supplemental Program

COMPUTER-BASED SKILLS PRACTICE AND ASSESSMENT REHEARSAL

➤ Standards-aligned workbooks

➤ Practice tests that mirror state assessments

➤ Fifteen tech-enhanced items practice

➤ Resource recommendations such as apps, books, & videos

➤ Personalized learning assignments for students

Call us for more information

888 - 309 - 8227

lumoslearning.com/a/online-program

Trusted by over 60,000 Students, 600 Schools, & 6000 Teachers

PARTIAL CUSTOMER LIST

Other Books in SkillBuilder Series

Reading Comprehension SkillBuilder
- Literature
- Informational Text
- Evidence-based Reading

English Language and Grammar SkillBuilder
- Conventions
- Vocabulary
- Knowledge of Language

Fractions and Base Ten SkillBuilder
- Addition & Subtraction
- Fractions of a Whole

Measurement, Representation, Interpretation and Geometry SkillBuilder
- Time
- Liquid Volume & Mass
- 2-Dimensional Shapes

http://lumoslearning.com/a/sbtb